NORSE MYTHOLOGY ALL ABOUT VIKINGS

Speedy Publishing LLC
40 E. Main St. #1156
Newark, DE 19711
www.speedypublishing.com

The Vikings were some of the Norse people who originated from northern Europe.

The Vikings were a
seafaring people from
the late eighth to
early 11th century who
established a name for
themselves as traders,
explorers and warriors.

Facilitated by advanced seafaring skills, and characterised by the longship, Viking activities at times also extended into the Mediterranean littoral, North Africa, the Middle East and Central Asia.

They discovered the
Americas long before
Columbus and could be
found as far east as the
distant reaches of Russia.

The Viking Age references
the earliest recorded
raid in the 790s until
the Norman Conquest
of England in 1066.

Viking people were very
keen on maintaining
personal hygiene.

Vikings also bathed at least once a week, much more frequently than other Europeans of their day.

While raiding proved
an excellent source of
income, many of the
Vikings held farms back
in their homeland.

When the men returned home from a raid, they resumed their normal routine of farming.

Vikings buried their
dead in boats.

In the Norse religion,
valiant warriors entered
festive and glorious realms
after death, and it was
thought that the vessels
that served them well in
life would help them reach
their final destinations.

When important Vikings
died, they would be placed
with all their clothes,
jewellery, even their
animals, in a burial ship.

This would either be
covered with a huge mound
of earth or set alight
and pushed out to sea.

The Vikings are remembered in history for their brutal raids.

Berserkers was the name
of some terrifying Viking
warriors who wore bear or
wolf skins and howled in
battle like wild animals.

The early Norse people
followed a pagan faith.
They believed in many
different Gods.

The Gods lived in Asgard,
which was connected to the
human earth by a rainbow
bridge. Odin, the Allfather,
was the chief God.

Odin's son Thor was the
God of thunder and carried
a powerful hammer.

Loki, a cheeky mischief-maker who could shape-shift to become all different kinds of animals.